Collins

easy learning

Grammar and punctuation

Ages 7–9

The cat **quietly** slept **on** the chair

adverb

preposition

How to use this book

- Find a quiet, comfortable place to work, away from distractions.
- Tackle one topic at a time.
- Help with reading the instructions where necessary and ensure your child understands what to do.
- Encourage your child to check their own answers as they complete each activity.
- Discuss with your child what they have learnt.
- Let your child return to their favourite pages once they have been completed, to talk about the activities.
- Reward your child with plenty of praise and encouragement.

Special features

- Yellow boxes: Introduce a topic and outline the key grammar or punctuation ideas.
- Red boxes: Emphasise a rule relating to the unit.
- Orange shaded boxes: Offer advice to parents on how to consolidate your child's understanding.

Published by Collins
An imprint of HarperCollins*Publishers*
1 London Bridge Street
London SE1 9GF

Browse the complete Collins catalogue at
www.collins.co.uk

© HarperCollins*Publishers* 2012
This edition © HarperCollins*Publishers* 2015

10 9 8 7

ISBN- 978-0-00-813422-8

Printed in Great Britain by Bell and Bain Ltd,
Glasgow

British Library Cataloguing in Publication Data

A Catalogue record for this publication is available from the British Library

Contributor: Rachel Grant
Page design by G Brasnett, Cambridge and Contentra Technologies
Illustrated by Kathy Baxendale, Steve Evans and Rachel Annie Bridgen
Cover design by Sarah Duxbury and Paul Oates
Cover illustration © Tomacco/Shutterstock
Project managed by Chantal Peacock and Sonia Dawkins

Contents

Phrases

Phrases are small groups of words.
Phrases don't make sense on their own.
Phrases usually don't have a verb.

The ball was kicked **over the hedge**.

over the hedge is a phrase.

A **noun phrase** contains a **noun**.

     the man

An **expanded noun phrase** tells us more about the **noun**.

     the tall, thin man

1   Which of the following are phrases? Write the phrases below.

in the kitchen   It began to rain.   The girls chatted.

along the beach   **He had to wait.**   **through the keyhole**

_____

_____

_____

2   Turn the nouns in these sentences into expanded noun phrases.

The _____ friends played with the _____ ball.

A _____ kite was flying high in the _____ sky.

3   Write the phrases into your own sentences.

through the village

_____

on the phone

_____

Ensure that your child spends time looking at the difference between a sentence and a phrase. It is important they recognise what a phrase is.

Main clauses

A **main clause** is a group of words that is the main part of a **sentence** and could be a **sentence** by itself.

> Our sheep love apples, though too many makes them ill.
>
> subject = Our sheep   verb = love

A **main clause** (underlined) must contain a *subject* (main thing or person) and *a verb*.

1 Write down the subject and verb in each of the underlined main clauses.

Mum weighed flour and eggs for the cake which she was making.

_____   _____

I rode a bike before my seventh birthday.

_____   _____

These toys are cheap but they last a long time.

_____   _____

2 Write these subjects and verbs into a main clause.

> deer   ate

_____

> sister   annoyed

_____

3 Underline the main clause in these sentences.

The dentist pulled out one of my teeth, after giving me an injection.

He left his gloves on the bus on his way to work.

Ensure your child knows the difference between phrases (covered on p. 4) and the clauses covered in this topic. Phrases are usually short and do not contain a verb. Main clauses contain a verb and can be a sentence in their own right.

Verbs 1

A **verb** is usually a doing word.

The present tense tells us what is happening now.

     Tyler **kicks** the ball. (**present tense**)

We can also write the present tense like this.

     Tyler is **kicking** the ball. (**present continuous tense**)

This shows a continuous action that is happening now.

The past tense tells us what has already happened.

     Tyler **kicked** the ball. (**past tense**)

We can also write the past tense like this.

     Tyler **was kicking** the ball. (**past continuous tense**)

This shows a continuous action that happened in the past.

1 Complete the sentences with a verb from the box.

> **bought**   **broke**   **is licking**   **was sitting**   **mows**

Dan _____ his ice cream quickly.

Dad _____ the lawn every Saturday.

Sarah _____ a newspaper at lunchtime.

The swing _____ when Jay _____ on it.

2 Complete the table with present continuous and past continuous tense.

Present tense	Present continuous tense	Past tense	Past continuous tense
He skips		She painted	
She shouts		I wrote	
They sleep		We drank	

Mime some actions and ask your child to write the 'action' word you are miming. Then ask him/her to write the verb in the past tense. This might highlight the fact that verbs can be regular (smile, smiled) or irregular (sing, sang).

Statements and commands

A **statement** is a sentence that contains information. A **statement** usually ends in a full stop.

>   I'm going to my room.

A **command** is a sentence that tells someone to do something.
A **command** can end in a full stop or an exclamation mark.

>   Go to your room, now!

If the command is forceful, we usually use an exclamation mark. If the command is not forceful, use a full stop.

>   Put your books away, please.

1   Write a statement that answers these questions.

What is your name?

_____

Where are you going after school?

_____

When is your birthday?

_____

2   Write a command for each of the following verbs.

wash   _____

take   _____

tell   _____

Questions

A **question** begins with a **capital letter** and ends with a **question mark**.

What shall we do today?

Questions help us to find out things.

1 Write three questions you would like to ask an adult. Write down who you are going to ask. (Hint: It might be your teacher, the Queen or your aunty.)

Who my questions are for: _____

My questions: _____

_____

_____

2 Write a question for each of these answers.

I'm going to take my coat.

_____

We are going to a restaurant.

_____

Yes, I'll buy some milk on the way home.

_____

We will arrive in the morning at about 11 am.

_____

Discuss different types of questions with your child. Closed questions can be answered with a 'yes' or 'no'. Open questions have a variety of different answers. Think of a famous person and ask your child to ask closed questions to discover who it might be.

Exclamations

This is an **exclamation mark** !
It can be used at the end of a **sentence** to show *shock, fear, pain, danger, humour, surprise, joy, anger* or *a command*.

Ouch, I fell over**!**

1 Complete the table with the exclamations.
Remember to add the exclamation marks.

Don't touch

Quick, get over here

Watch out

That hurt

Ouch, please don't

Pain!	Surprise!	An order!

Help, I've hurt my foot

I don't believe it

Stop, right now

Wow, look at that

2 Write an example of each type of exclamation.

shock _____

anger _____

upset _____

joy _____

Show your child different facial expressions, then ask them to write an exclamation that might go with each one.

Subject-verb agreement

The **subject** of a sentence is often a **noun** or **pronoun**.
The **subject** is the person or thing that is *doing* or *being* something in the sentence.
It is important when you write sentences that the **subject** *agrees with* the **verb**. This is called **subject-verb agreement**.
When the **subject** is singular, the **verb** must also be in the singular form.
When the **subject** is plural, the **verb** must also be in the plural form.

This cold ice lolly is so refreshing! **Fruit flavours are** my favourite.

1 Circle the mistake in each sentence. Then write the correct word at the end of each sentence.

Seagulls was swooping through the square. _____

The children has been very quiet all morning. _____

Dad leave for work very early every morning. _____

Next week I are singing in the school performance. _____

2 Complete each sentence by writing the correct form of the verb. The verb is given in brackets.

The teacher _____ her bike to school each day. (ride)

Pets _____ not allowed at the hotel. (be)

Most of the book _____ really boring but

I _____ enjoying the ending. (be)

They all _____ happy about the result. (feel)

3 Complete the sentences for each of these subjects. Make sure your verbs agree with the subjects.

Ella and Jason _____

Our school playground_____

Explain to your child that in everyday speech and some informal contexts, it is accepted that subject and verb sometimes disagree. However, in standard written English the subject and verb should always agree.

Determiners

A **determiner** is a word that comes before a **noun**.
It tells us if the **noun** is specific or general.
Articles are the most common types of **determiner**.

Other **determiners** are
this, that, these and **those**.

the is the **definite article**. We use it to refer to specific things.

a and **an** are **indefinite articles**. We use them to refer to general things.

It is important to know if **a** or **an** is needed in front of a word.
a is used in front of words beginning with a consonant or a consonant sound.

an is usually used in front of words beginning with a vowel or a silent **h**.
The letters **a e i o u** are vowels.

The mouse ran out of **a** hole and disappeared into **an** old shed.

1 Add **a** or **an** in front of these nouns.

_____ jacket   _____ book   _____ hour

_____ egg   _____ scarf   _____ igloo

_____ apple   _____ cake   _____ oven

_____ octopus   _____ animal   _____ gate

2 Underline all the determiners in these sentences.

The young woman was reading an interesting book about a journey.

He told the worried man that he would give him a hand.

This path is definitely the right way to get back to the house.

Could I borrow that pen for a moment? This one is broken.

3 Write two nouns from **1** and two adjectives from **2** into two different sentences.

_____

_____

Inverted commas

Inverted commas (" ... ") are sometimes called speech marks. We use them to show the exact words someone has spoken.

What the person says is written inside the **inverted commas**.

The final punctuation goes inside the **inverted commas**. It may be a **comma**, a **question mark** or an **exclamation mark**.

"I am going to the park**,**" said James.

"Are you going to the park**?**" asked James.

1 Write down what is said in the speech bubbles using inverted commas.

It is time to leave.

"_____,"said Abby.

Do we have to?

"_____?"said Dom.

Yes, or we will be late.

"_____,"said Abby.

2 Abby and Dom then go home and see their Mum.
Finish the conversation between Abby, Dom and their Mum.
Remember to put the final punctuation inside the inverted commas.

"_____" said Dom.

"_____" said Mum.

"_____" said Abby.

"_____" said Dom.

Highlight to your child the link between speech bubbles and inverted commas. Inverted commas show the exact words spoken including all punctuation. Have a silent conversation with your child – the two of you need to write everything down on paper using inverted commas!

Prepositions 1

Prepositions show relationships between **nouns** (or **pronouns**) and other words in the **sentence**.

They often indicate *position* or *time*.

The cat slept **in** the box.

He's been there **since** this morning.

1 Circle the preposition in each sentence.

The muddy dog jumped in the puddle.

Kylie sat beside her brother.

I fell asleep during the film.

The walkers climbed up the hill.

2 Add a preposition to each of the sentences.

The old man walked _____ the bridge.

Garry swam _____ the icy pool.

Meena likes to have a nap _____ lunch.

Toby jumped _____ the wall.

3 Write your own sentences using the prepositions.

inside _____

behind _____

since _____

into _____

With your child look for the word 'position' in the word 'preposition'. Link it with part of the definition of a preposition (i.e. 'prepositions' often indicate 'position').

Conjunctions 1

Two **sentences** can be joined by adding a word between them.
The *joining word* is called a **conjunction.**

> Tom tripped on the kerb. He didn't hurt himself.
> Tom tripped on the kerb **but** he didn't hurt himself.

Conjunctions are sometimes called **connectives**.

1 The words in the box can all be conjunctions.
Copy and join each pair of sentences using a different conjunction.

however	or	so	as	because	but	yet	and	when

Darren tried to call Gareth. His phone had no service.

_____

Sunita climbed to the top of a tree. She wasn't scared at all.

_____

John was very hungry. He hadn't had any breakfast.

_____

2 Complete these sentences.

The radio played Kate's favourite song **but** _____

_____

Alex will finish his homework **when** _____

_____

3 Write your own sentence using this conjunction.

so _____

Give your child other conjunctions (as shown in **1**) and ask them to write sentences using them.

Conjunctions 2

A **conjunction** can also link two **words**, **phrases**, or **clauses** together in a **sentence**.
Some **conjunctions** link two things that are of equal importance.

Steve likes coffee **and** tea.

Some **conjunctions** link a **main clause** and a **subordinate clause**.
The **subordinate clause** only works when it is linked with the **main clause**.
The **subordinate clause** does not make sense on its own.

I had no idea it was raining **until** I looked out of the window.

1 Add the missing conjunctions to these sentences using the words in the box.

| since | unless | until | whenever |

Adele played really well _____ she hurt her leg.

_____ it's so hot, why don't we buy some ice cream for tea?

_____ I play the piano, I feel more relaxed.

I can't watch the football _____ I finish my homework.

2 Complete these sentences. You must use a conjunction.

Help yourself to anything in the fridge _____

I don't have much free time _____

3 Write your own sentences using these conjunctions.

unless _____

yet _____

Encourage your child to recognise how different conjunctions give different meanings to a sentence:
when indicates time, **because** points to a reason, **although** indicates a contrast, etc. Also see
Subordinate clauses (p. 28).

Pronouns 1

Pronouns are used instead of **nouns**.
Pronouns avoid repeating **nouns** in **sentences**.

Tim walked the dog before *Tim* went to meet *Tim's* friends.
Tim walked the dog before **he** went to meet **his** friends.

1 Use the pronouns in the box to complete the sentences.

> **I**   it   we   you   them

Jay said _____ was his book.

The teacher asked _____ if their boots were clean.

_____ love to eat hot chips.

Can _____ go to the Ice Show?

Did _____ see who made that mess?

2 Underline the pronouns in the sentences.

They loved performing and the parents watched them with pride.

"The saucepan is hot," she said.

It frightened me.

He came to visit us but we were out.

3 Copy the sentence, replacing the <u>underlined</u> words with a pronoun.

Laila looked forward to seeing <u>the boy</u> each weekend.

_____

Subject and object

The **subject** of a **sentence** is *who* or *what* the sentence is about.
The **object** of a **sentence** is the person or thing having something done to it.

For example, in the sentence, 'I love you', I is the subject (the person doing the loving) and you is the object (the person being loved).

You can find the subject of a sentence by first finding the verb.

1 Underline the subject and circle the object in these sentences.

The cat chased the mouse.

Snow fell on the ground.

She explained the game.

The little girl played the piano.

2 Write sentences for these pairs of subjects and objects.

Kasim   kiwi fruit

_____

shaggy dog   juicy bone

_____

traffic warden   parking ticket

_____

3 Write a subject and an object to complete these sentences.

_____ enjoy _____.

_____ watched _____.

Verbs 2

A **verb** in the past tense tells us what has already happened.

  Tyler **kicked** the ball. (**past tense**)

We can also write the past tense like this.

  Tyler **has kicked** the ball. (**present perfect tense**)

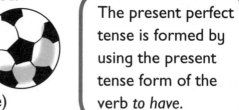

The present perfect tense is formed by using the present tense form of the verb *to have*.

This tells us about an action that happened at an unspecified time in the past.

1 Complete these sentences. Write the verbs in the present perfect tense.

The lions _____ (chase) the buffalo.

Jamie _____ (not feel) very well.

Janine _____ (is) a great gymnast.

The children _____ (leave) for school.

2 Write sentences of your own using the present perfect tense, as listed below.

have played   _____

has told   _____

have made   _____

has slept   _____

3 Complete the sentences using a verb in the present perfect tense.

We _____ delicious sweets.

The teacher _____ how to do the experiment.

Since spring, the lambs _____ their mothers.

With your child look for examples of verbs in the present perfect tense in their reading book. Encourage them to notice the difference in meaning between the present perfect tense and the past continuous tense (see p. 6).

Adverbs 1

Adverbs tell us more about **verbs**.
Many adverbs end with the suffix **ly**.

> Alan **excitedly** opened his presents.

Adverbs tell us how, when, where or how often
something happens or is done.

1 Look carefully at the sentences. Circle the adverb in each one.

The mother gently rocked her baby.

Kylie sang beautifully.

We occasionally have fish and chips for tea.

We quickly ran for the bus.

2 Use each of these adverbs in your own sentences.

sensibly _____

angrily _____

quietly _____

fiercely _____

3 Complete the table with adverbs that can be used with these verbs.

walk	draw	argue	eat

Adverbs 2

Adverbial phrases give us more information about a verb.
Adverbial phrases tell us when, where or how often something happens or is done.
When an adverbial phrase is placed at the start of a sentence, it is known as a
fronted adverbial. We usually put a comma after it.

Every now and again, she stroked the sleeping cat.

Before I go to bed, I always brush my teeth.

1 Underline the adverbial phrases in these sentences.

As the sun went down, the sky burned a brilliant orange.

When we heard the bang, we woke up and ran to the window.

Later that day, we found him in the park.

With a huge smile, he opened the present.

2 Match the adverbial phrases to make sentences.

Every now and then,   I saw a beautiful butterfly.

Until yesterday,   I go swimming with Dave.

While I was in the garden,   I didn't know you had a sister.

3 Write sentences of your own using these phrases.
Each sentence must contain an adverbial phrase.

in the middle of the night

with nervous little steps

_____

Prepositions 2

Prepositions show relationships between **nouns** (or **pronouns**) and other words in the sentence. They often indicate position or time.

The cat walked **on** the table.
He's been there **since** this morning.

1 List the prepositions found in this passage.

Jess searched in the wardrobe and under the bed. She searched all morning. She hunted inside the cupboard and looked through all the drawers. It must be here somewhere! Perhaps it was behind the curtain…

_____   _____   _____   _____   _____

2 Finish the sentences with a preposition and ending.

Daniel jumped _____

Hannah slept _____

The teacher looked _____

The snow lay _____

3 Write your own sentences using the prepositions.

among _____

beyond _____

in _____

The following words are all prepositions: towards, upon, beyond, by, near, within, past, off, inside, into, behind, above, about, on, across, against, at, among, beside. Ask your child to make a list of all the prepositions they can think of.

Direct speech 1

Inverted commas or speech marks (" …") show the exact words someone has spoken. This is called direct speech.

"Does the film start at 3 o'clock?" asked Sonia.

What the person says is written inside **inverted commas**. The final punctuation goes inside the inverted commas. It may be a comma, a question mark or an exclamation mark.

1 Copy the sentences. Add the missing punctuation.

I wish this lesson would finish said Tuhil

_____

Why asked Mark

_____

I am starving and want my lunch answered Tuhil

_____

Didn't you have a snack earlier said Mark

_____

2 Write a conversation between two friends.
Remember to use inverted commas and correct punctuation.

_____ asked _____

_____ answered _____

_____ exclaimed _____

_____ whispered_____

_____ agreed _____

Pronouns 2

Pronouns are used instead of **nouns**.
Pronouns avoid repeating nouns in **sentences**.

Veejay's dad bought *Veejay* a new puppy.
Veejay's dad bought **him** a new puppy.

Pronouns can be singular or plural.
A **possessive pronoun** shows ownership.

Veejay loves **his** new puppy.

1 Circle the pronouns.

him   it   when   behind   we   where   them   their   on   you

2 Complete the table with the words from the box.

yours   me   us   mine   they   theirs

Pronouns	Possessive pronouns

3 Copy the sentences, replacing the <u>underlined</u> words with pronouns so they make sense.

Tom jumped in a puddle so <u>Tom</u> could splash his brother.

_____

Finn and Ben are twins and people often get <u>Finn and Ben's</u> names mixed up.

_____

Lucy has a puppy and <u>Lucy</u> enjoys playing with <u>her puppy</u>.

_____

Direct speech 2

When we write **direct speech** we use **inverted commas** to show the exact words that someone said.

"I never agreed to getting a dog," Mum said.

In direct speech the punctuation always goes inside the closing **inverted commas**.

When we write **reported speech**, we report what someone said. We do not use **inverted commas**. We use *that* to introduce what was said.

Mum said **that** she had never agreed to getting a dog.

1 These sentences are in reported speech. Change them into direct speech.

The forecaster said that there will be heavy snow later.

_____

My coach said that I need to improve.

_____

Sadie replied that she had already seen the film.

_____

2 Add inverted commas and other missing punctuation in the correct places.

What do you want for supper asked Mum

I'm not really hungry Jo replied

Well you need to eat something Mum replied You've been out all day

I'll just have a sandwich later said Jo Is there any cheese left

I think Christa has eaten it all Mum replied

Greedy guts said Jo

Ask your child to find examples of reported speech and direct speech in a magazine article such as an interview. Practise changing direct speech to reported speech and reported speech to direct speech.

Comparative and superlative adjectives

Adjectives are describing words.

A **comparative adjective** compares two **nouns**. Many **comparative adjectives** end in **er**.

A **superlative adjective** compares three or more nouns. Many **superlative adjectives** end in **est**.

big   bigger   biggest

1 Complete the sentences with words from the box.

> long   longer   longest   hot   hotter   hottest

My drink is _____, Mum's is _____

but Dad's is the _____.

Deena's daisy chain is _____, Becky's is

_____ but Heidi's is the _____.

2 Complete the table. **Remember** to check your spellings.

Adjective	Comparative	Superlative
small		
		wettest
	softer	
large		
		prettiest

3 Write these adjectives into a sentence.   **busy   busier   busiest**

_____

_____

Apostrophes

An **apostrophe** can show when someone owns something.

One owner = noun + **'s**	Kate**'s**
More than one owner = noun + **'s**	children**'s**
More than one owner **but** noun ending in **s** = noun + **'**	girls**'**

1 These are all singular nouns. Copy the phrase and add the missing apostrophe.

the builders hat _____

the horses saddle _____

the nurses thermometer _____

the climbers rope _____

2 These are all plural nouns. Copy the phrase and add the missing apostrophe.

the animals food _____

the childrens sweets _____

the flowers stems _____

the policemens helmets _____

3 Write each phrase into a sentence. **Remember** to add the missing apostrophe.

Bens books

_____

cats kittens

_____

Apostrophes used for possession is a very difficult topic for children to grasp. Work through the rules found on this page with your child. Discourage your child from adding an apostrophe every time they see a plural noun ending in s, and emphasise that they only need an apostrophe when they see an s to show possession.

Conjunctions 3

Conjunctions are *joining* words.

It was a strange **and** scary story.

Some conjunctions can be used at the start of a sentence to show the relationship between ideas in writing.

Some conjunctions are:
- also, furthermore (to show addition)
- besides, after all (to show reinforcement)
- before, at first, meanwhile, in the meantime, finally (to show time or sequence)
- however (to show opposition)
- for example, such as (to explain)
- therefore, as a result (to show results)

1 Complete these sentences using conjunctions from the box.

> **at last**   **therefore**   **furthermore**   **at first**

We waited for thirty minutes. _____, the coach appeared – and we were off!

That building is ugly. _____, it was very expensive to build.

_____ I was nervous, but once I started speaking, my nerves disappeared.

The canteen will be closed on Monday. _____, you will need to bring a packed lunch.

2 What is the conjunction showing in each of these sentences? Choose a function from the box. Write the function at the end of each sentence.

> **to show opposition**   **to explain**   **to show time or sequence**

For example, running shorts and a T-shirt may be worn.   _____

Meanwhile, beat the egg whites until stiff.   _____

However, if it is wet, the party will take place indoors.   _____

3 Write your own sentences using these conjunctions.

As a result, _____

Besides, _____

Subordinate clauses

We can join two **main clauses** with a **conjunction**.

I love to eat apples **but** I don't like oranges.

Subordinate clauses are also introduced by a **conjunction**.
A **subordinate clause** only makes sense with a **main clause**. It could not be a sentence by itself.

We need to wrap up warm **because** the weather is snowy.

We can also place the **subordinate clause** before the **main clause**. When we do this, we must add a **comma** after the **subordinate clause**.

Because the weather is snowy, we need to wrap up warm.

1 Underline the subordinate clause in these sentences.

Although he was tired, the teacher tidied the classroom.

The dog chased after the ball while my grandfather watched.

Because it was hungry, the lion pounced on its prey.

2 Use these phrases to make sentences that contain a main clause and a subordinate clause.

stops raining   go out to play

_____

felt ill   went to school

_____

3 Circle the main clause and underline the subordinate clause in each of these sentences.

Your teeth will fall out if you don't brush them regularly!

My book fell out of my bag because I was rushing to school.

Ensure your child knows the difference between main clauses and subordinate clauses. Every clause must contain a subject and a verb. A main clause makes sense on its own. A subordinate clause needs a main clause to help it make sense (see p. 5).

Grammar and punctuation terms

Grammar and punctuation terms are the words we use to talk about the rules of grammar and punctuation.

Preposition, conjunction, main clause, subordinate clause, determiner, pronoun, possessive pronoun and adverbial are all grammar terms.

Inverted commas is a punctuation term.

1 Match each highlighted word or phrase in this sentence to one of the grammar or punctuation terms listed above. Write the terms in the boxes.

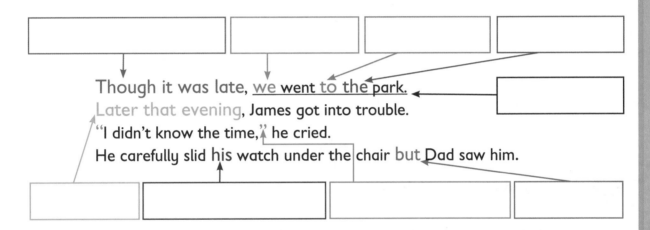

2 Draw lines to match each grammar and punctuation term to its correct definition.

conjunction	Marks the beginning and end of direct speech.
clause	Tells us when, where or how often something happens.
determiner	Shows the relationship between words in a sentence.
adverbial	A word that introduces a noun.
inverted commas	A group of words that includes a subject and a verb.
preposition	A word that joins two parts of a sentence.

How am I doing?

The next two pages revise many grammar and punctuation subjects covered in this book.

If you get stuck, look back at earlier topics.

1 Copy the sentences.
Add the missing **inverted commas**.

Are we nearly there yet? asked Tuhil.

_____

It is freezing outside, said Jake.

_____

I feel very tired tonight, yawned Meg.

_____

2 Add **a** or **an** in front of the nouns.

_____ dog	_____ elephant	_____ bucket
_____ cup	_____ icebox	_____ hour
_____ lock	_____ angel	_____ towel
_____ explorer	_____ icicle	_____ wagon

3 Add an **adverb** to each of the sentences.

The children played _____.

The trees blew _____ in the wind.

Fiona slept _____ despite the storm.

I ran _____ to get help.

4 Add the missing punctuation.

Thats fantastic news

Where are we going to eat

Go and tidy your room

5 Complete the table with words from the sentence.

The sheep raced into the lush field and they quickly started to eat the grass.

noun	verb	adjective	preposition	pronoun	conjunction

6 Copy the phrase and add the missing apostrophe.

the lions cub _____

the childrens parents _____

the teachers car park _____

7 Find the verb in each sentence and write down the correct form.

Look! The sun are coming out! _____

His hair have been cut very short. _____

They was aware of someone following them. _____

Some of the marbles is on the floor. _____

Hannah is someone who like to read comics. _____

8 Write the comparative and superlative adjectives for each of the adjectives.

old _____ _____

red _____ _____

Go back to the topics that your child still finds tricky.

Answers

Phrases
Page 4

1. in the kitchen
   along the beach
   through the keyhole

2. Child to complete sentences with an expanded noun phrase.

3. Child's own sentences using the given phrases.

Main clauses
Page 5

1. Mum – weighed
   I – rode
   toys – are

2. Child's own sentences using the given subjects and verbs.

3. <u>The dentist pulled out one of my teeth</u>, after giving me an injection.
   <u>He left his gloves on the bus</u> on his way to work.

Verbs 1
Page 6

1. Dan is licking his ice cream quickly.
   Dad mows the lawn every Saturday.
   Sarah bought a newspaper at lunchtime.
   The swing broke when Jay was sitting on it.

2.

Present continuous tense
he is skipping
she is shouting
they are sleeping

Past continuous tense
she was painting
I was writing
we were drinking

Statements and commands
Page 7

1. Child's own statements.

2. Child's own commands using listed verbs.

Questions
Page 8

1. Child's three questions written for a named adult.

2. e.g. Are you going to be warm enough?
   e.g. Where are we going for tea?
   e.g. Will you buy some milk?
   e.g. What time are you arriving?

Exclamations
Page 9

1.

Pain!	Surprise!	An order!
That hurt!	I don't believe it!	Don't touch!
Help, I've hurt my foot!	Watch out!	Quick, get over here!
Ouch, please don't!	Wow, look at that!	Stop, right now!

2. Child's own examples of exclamations.

Subject-verb agreement
Page 10

1. (was) were
   (has) have
   (leave) leaves
   (are) am

2. rides
   are
   is/was – am
   feel/felt

3. Child's own sentences.

Determiners
Page 11

1. a jacket, a book, an hour, an egg, a scarf, an igloo, an apple, a cake, an oven, an octopus, an animal, a gate

2. the – an – a
   the – that – a
   this – the – the
   that – a – this

3. Child's own sentences using nouns from **1** and adjectives from **2**.

Inverted commas
Page 12

1. "It is time to leave," said Abby.
   "Do we have to?" said Dom.
   "Yes, or we will be late," said Abby.

2. The child continues the conversation between Abby, Dom and Mum.

Prepositions 1
Page 13

1. The muddy dog jumped (in) the puddle.
   Kylie sat (beside) her brother.
   I fell asleep (during) the film.
   The walkers climbed (up) the hill.

2. e.g. The old man walked *across* the bridge.
   e.g. Garry swam *in* the icy pool.
   e.g. Meena likes to have a nap *after/before* lunch.
   e.g. Toby jumped *over* the wall.

3. The child's own sentences using the given prepositions.

Conjunctions 1
Page 14

1. e.g. Darren tried to call Gareth but his phone had no service.
   e.g. Sunita climbed to the top of a tree however she wasn't scared at all.
   e.g. John was very hungry because he hadn't had any breakfast.

2. Child's own sentences.

3. A sentence written using the conjunction **so**.

Conjunctions 2
Page 15

1. until
   since
   whenever
   unless

2. Two of child's own sentences that include a conjunction and use a subordinate clause.

3. Two of child's own sentences using the given conjunctions.

Pronouns 1
Page 16

1. Jay said <u>it</u> was his book.
   The teacher asked <u>them</u> if their boots were clean.
   <u>I/We</u> love to eat hot chips.
   Can <u>we/I/you</u> go to the Ice Show?
   Did <u>you</u> see who made that mess?

2. <u>They</u> loved performing and the parents watched <u>them</u> with pride.
   "The saucepan is hot," <u>she</u> said.
   <u>It</u> frightened <u>me</u>.
   <u>He</u> came to visit <u>us</u> but <u>we</u> were out.

3. Laila looked forward to seeing <u>him</u> each weekend.

Subject and object
Page 17

1. subject: the cat – object: the mouse
   subject: snow – object: ground
   subject: she – object: the game
   subject: the little girl – object: the piano

2. Child's own sentences.

3. Child's own sentences.

Verbs 2
Page 18

1. have chased
   has not felt
   has been
   have left

2. Child's own sentences using the present perfect tense.

3. Child completes the sentences using the present perfect tense.